CW00797954

The SOUTH AFRICAN
AIR FRYER
COOKBOOK

LOUISA HOLST

First published in 2022 by Human & Rousseau
An imprint of NB Publishers, a Division of Media24 Boeke (Pty) Ltd
40 Heerengracht, Cape Town 8001

First edition, fourth impression 2023

Copyright © published edition: Human & Rousseau (2022)
Copyright © text: Louisa Holst (2022)
No part of this book may be reproduced or transmitted in any form or
by any electronic or mechanical means, including photocopying and
recording, or by any other information storage or retrieval system,
without written permission from the publisher.

Publisher: Lindy Samery
Editor: Diana Procter
Proofreader: Glynne Newlands
Designer: Wilna Combrinck
Photographer: Donna Lewis
Creative director and stylist: Hannes Koegelenberg
Food preparation: Louisa Holst and Gilionelle Kaba
Index: Anna Tanneberger

Printed by **novus print**, a division of Novus Holdings

ISBN: 978-0-7981-8332-1

Special thanks to the Clicks group for sponsoring the air fryers.
We prepared our recipes in a 5,5 litre Kambrook Aspire Digital Health
Air Fryer, available at Clicks stores nationwide.

CONTENTS

INTRODUCTION

I remember being so excited when I bought my first air fryer a few years ago; everyone was talking about this amazing appliance and they all said I HAD to have one! However, once I had it, I was not really sure how to use it. For a long time, it was basically a potato chip-making machine and useful for reheating leftovers. I slowly started experimenting and trying out different recipes, and it was then that I realised that an air fryer is really quite a useful gadget.

It has many benefits – it saves you time because things cook much quicker than in an oven and, because an air fryer uses rapid air technology to create heat, it heats up faster than an oven. In this way it saves you money because it uses a lot less electricity than a large oven. It is easy to use, making it more likely that teens will get involved and help with the cooking. If you are only cooking for one or two, it's a must-have. It is also much healthier than deep-frying. I like to use a little oil to drizzle or spray onto the ingredients, just to keep them crisp and golden, but this is still a fraction of what you would use if you were deep-frying.

Experiment with your air fryer and try out different ingredients. You will soon see what works and what doesn't. Fattier ingredients like chicken wings and pork rashers work well, resulting in succulent meat and deliciously crisp skin. If you are using a leaner cut of meat or chicken, make sure you don't overcook it – use a marinade or glaze to keep it juicy.

Baking is also possible in the air fryer, although on a smaller scale as the size of the basket limits you to what you can do. But you can bake a few muffins at a time so they are perfectly fresh for breakfast, or whip up a savoury bread to serve at your braai in half the normal time.

Use the cooking times in air fryer recipes as a guide: it is difficult to give exact times because there are many different makes and

models available, all with slightly different capabilities. You will soon learn how long it takes your specific air fryer to cook basic ingredients.

There are many fantastic, time-saving recipes that you can prepare in your air fryer and this collection will help you get off to a good start. I've included a selection ranging from snacks and easy weeknight meals to wholesome family suppers, vegetable dishes and delightful desserts and bakes. There are also many South African favourites and lekker local flavours. The recipes are no-fuss, delicious, quick and easy to prepare, and designed to help you make the most of your air fryer. I hope you enjoy them and find a few favourites that will make your life a little easier and dinner time a lot tastier!

TIPS FOR AIR-FRYING SUCCESS

- Not all recipes specify that you need to preheat your air fryer before cooking, but I prefer to do it. It shortens the cooking time and ensures good results, especially when you are cooking meat or baking. Check the instructions for your air fryer – some will beep when they have reached the correct heat and others have a light that goes on or off.
- Don't overload your air fryer's basket and never fill it more than two-thirds full. It is better to cook one layer of ingredients at a time to make sure that the air can circulate properly and the food is able to crisp and brown.
- Turn or toss your ingredients halfway through cooking. Most ingredients, especially vegetables and chips, need to be tossed during cooking to ensure that they cook and crisp up evenly. Sometimes bakes need to be rotated if your air fryer doesn't cook evenly.
- Use a meat thermometer to check if your meat is cooked through, especially if you are cooking larger cuts of meat, especially pork. In general, most things will cook much quicker in the air fryer compared to the oven.
- Bakes, especially smaller bakes like cupcakes, sometimes finish up with a wobbly shape. This is due to the air that blows on them during cooking, as well as the fact that the element at the top of the air fryer is quite close to the batter. You can cover your bakes with a piece of aluminium foil to help create a better shape.
- If you are cooking very fatty ingredient like pork rashers, you may notice a lot of smoke coming out of the air vents in your air fryer. To help reduce the smoke, pour a little water into the base of your air fryer under the basket.
- Always make sure that your air fryer has space around it. It is necessary for the air to circulate as this helps it not to overheat. It should also be on a heatproof surface.
- Always wash your air fryer after it has been used. Soak the basket and drawer in warm, soapy water. The non-stick surface should make cleaning with a soft sponge very easy. Some are also dishwasher safe but check the manual to make sure, otherwise the non-stick surface may get damaged and peel.

- Cooking times and temperatures differ to those of a conventional oven so you need to adapt your recipes. In general, you need to decrease the temperatures by about 20 °C and shorten the cooking times by about a quarter to half.
- Do not cover the whole base of the air fryer's basket with a large cooking container or foil. The air needs to circulate in order for it to cook properly. Use a smaller cooking container or a perforated silicone cooking mat.
- Brush or spray your ingredients with a little oil before adding any spices. The oil will help the spices to stick to the ingredients, otherwise they might be blown off by the circulating air.
- Avoid cooking very light ingredients in the air fryer as the circulating air can cause them to fly up and stick to the cooking element and burn. Do not cover food with a piece of baking paper for the same reason: it will get blown onto the element and burn. If you need to cover the food, use a piece of aluminium foil and tuck it in under your ingredients slightly.
- We prepared our recipes in a 5,5 litre Kambrook Aspire Digital Health Air Fryer, available at Clicks stores nationwide.
- All the recipes in this book were cooked using the air-fry mode.

USEFUL AIR-FRYER ACCESSORIES

- Read the manual of your specific air fryer to check if any products are not suitable for using in the appliance. However, in most cases, silicone baking moulds, baking paper liners, aluminium foil containers and ovenproof dishes and tins are all suitable. You are limited by the size of your air fryer, however, so most containers need to be 15-20 cm or smaller to fit into the air-fryer basket.
- Make sure you use silicone-coated tongs or spatulas to lift or turn your ingredients without scratching the non-stick surface on the insides of the air fryer.
- Parchment liners and silicone mats make cleaning the air fryer a lot easier and are especially useful if you are cooking a dish that has a marinade or sauce on it.
- An oil spray bottle is handy to use to spray a little oil onto your food before cooking. This will help give the food a golden, crisp finish. Add a little water to the oil in the bottle to help prevent the oil from clogging.
- Have a look at homeware stores, baking shops, plastic shops, packaging shops, Chinese stores and Takealot.com to find a variety of containers and baking accessories that can be used in an air fryer.

Here are some of the accessories we used while preparing the food for this recipe book:

1. Silicone tongs
2. Round ovenproof baking dishes
3. Enamel baking dishes
4. 15-cm loose-bottomed pie tin
5 & 23. Parchment paper liners for air fryers
6. Silicone air-fryer mat
7. 15-cm grill rack with skewers
8. 10 x 15-cm aluminium foil containers
9 & 10. Aluminium foil tart tins

11 & 12. Disposable mini quiche containers
13. Disposable muffin or cupcake cups
14. Paper liners to use in silicone muffin holders
15. Aluminium foil
16. Paper liners to use in mini loaf tins
17. Disposable mini loaf tin
18. 9 x 20-cm aluminium foil loaf tin
19. Mini loaf tin

20. 15 x 20-cm aluminium foil container
21. Oil spray bottle
22. 15-cm cake tin

Online contacts: Takealot.com, thebakingtin.co.za, crazystore.co.za, pepstores.com, mambos.co.za

AIR-FRYER
COOKING TIMES

These are approximate cooking times and will vary depending on the model and make of your air fryer. Cooking time will also depend on how full the air fryer's basket is. Turn or toss your ingredients halfway through the cooking time, and check your ingredients towards the end of the cooking time to see if they should come out a bit sooner or stay in for a little longer.

NOTE: All the recipes in this book were cooked using the air-fry mode.

	Temperature	Time
Chicken		
Breast fillet	190 °C	10-15 minutes
Wings	190 °C	20-25 minutes
Whole breast	180 °C	22-25 minutes
Whole chicken	160 °C	45-60 minutes
Whole pieces (thighs and drumsticks)	180 °C	25-35 minutes
Fish and seafood		
Calamari	200 °C	4-5 minutes
Fish cakes	200 °C	12-15 minutes
Fish fillets	200 °C	8-12 minutes
Prawns	190 °C	10-12 minutes
Beef		
Boerewors or sausage	200 °C	10-12 minutes
Burger patties	180 °C	10-15 minutes
Meatballs	190 °C	7-10 minutes
Steak (250 g)	200 °C	15-20 minutes
Lamb and pork		
Bacon	180 °C	8-12 minutes
Lamb chops	200 °C	8-12 minutes
Lamb ribs	180 °C	25-30 minutes
Pork belly roast	190 °C	50-60 minutes
Pork chops with bone	200 °C	10-18 minutes
Pork fillet	200 °C	15-20 minutes
Pork rashers	200 °C	25-30 minutes
Pork sausage	190 °C	10-15 minutes
Precooked pork ribs	200 °C	10-15 minutes

Vegetables		
Asparagus	200 °C	4-6 minutes
Brinjal cubes	190 °C	10-15 minutes
Brussels sprouts	190 °C	12-15 minutes
Butternut cubes	180 °C	25-30 minutes
Carrot pieces	180 °C	12-15 minutes
Cauliflower	200 °C	10-12 minutes
Cherry tomatoes	200 °C	5-8 minutes
Courgettes	190 °C	8-12 minutes
Mushrooms	200 °C	8-10 minutes
Onions	200 °C	8-10 minutes
Patty pans	190 °C	10-12 minutes
Pumpkin cubes	180 °C	25-30 minutes
Sweetcorn on the cob	200 °C	10-12 minutes
Sweet peppers	190 °C	10-15 minutes
Potatoes		
Baby	190 °C	12-15 minutes
Potato cubes	190 °C	12-18 minutes
Whole	190 °C	40-50 minutes
Sweet potato wedges	180 °C	10-15 minutes
Whole sweet potatoes	180 °C	30-35 minutes
Ready-made foods		
Chicken burgers	180 °C	10-12 minutes
Chicken nuggets	190 °C	10-12 minutes
Chicken schnitzel	190 °C	10-12 minutes
Crumbed fish fillets	200 °C	10-12 minutes
Fish fingers	200 °C	12-15 minutes
Pastries	180 °C	12-20 minutes
Pizza	200 °C	10-12 minutes
Potato chips	190 °C	12-15 minutes
Potato wedges	190 °C	15-18 minutes
Sweet potato chips	190 °C	12-15 minutes
Waffles	180 °C	5-8 minutes
Bakes		
Bread	160 °C	30-40 minutes
Cakes	160 °C	30-40 minutes
Muffins and cupcakes	180 °C	12-15 minutes
Puddings	160 °C	25-40 minutes

SNACKS *and* STARTERS

FISH CAKES *with* ACHAR MAYONNAISE

🍴 Serves: 4-6

🕐 Preparation time: 30 minutes

🌡 Air-fryer temperature: 200 °C

⏱ Cooking time: 10-12 minutes

2 medium potatoes, boiled
2 x 170 g cans tuna in water, drained
3 large eggs
3 spring onions, chopped
5 ml grated lemon zest
Salt and freshly ground black pepper, to taste
70 g (125 ml) cake flour
250 ml dried breadcrumbs or panko crumbs
30 ml canola oil
125 ml mayonnaise
30 ml mango achar, chopped

Spice up your dipping sauce with a little mango achar. It turns an ordinary fish cake into a tasty treat.

1. Peel the potatoes and grate them into a bowl. Squeeze all the excess liquid from the tuna. Add the tuna, 2 of the eggs, the spring onions and lemon zest to the potatoes. Season with salt and freshly ground black pepper. Mix well, then shape the mixture into round patties.

2. Put the flour on a plate and the breadcrumbs or panko crumbs on another plate. Whisk the remaining egg. Dust each patty with flour, then dip into the egg. Allow the excess egg to run off and then cover with the crumbs.

3. Pour the oil onto a plate and roll each patty in a little oil, or spray with oil if you have an oil spray bottle.

4. Preheat the air fryer to 200 °C. Place the fish cakes into the basket and cook for 10-12 minutes at 200 °C. Turn the fish cakes over halfway through the cooking time. Stir the mayonnaise and achar together. Serve with the fish cakes.

CREAM CHEESE *and biltong* SPRING ROLLS

Filo pastry cooks quickly and easily in an air fryer. Try it out with these moreish pastries, which make a great pre-dinner snack or starter.

🍴 Serves: 4
🕐 Preparation time: 30 minutes
🌡️ Air-fryer temperature: 180 °C
⏱️ Cooking time: 8-10 minutes per batch

10 sheets filo pastry
50 ml melted butter
150 ml cream cheese
150 ml thinly sliced soft biltong (you can also use smoked ham, salami or cooked spinach as variations)
50 ml grated Cheddar cheese
2 spring onions, thinly sliced
4 piquanté peppers (Peppadews), sliced
Salt, to taste
sweet chilli sauce or chutney, to serve

1. Keep the filo pastry sheets covered with a damp tea towel while you work so they don't dry out. Brush one sheet with melted butter and then cover with another sheet. Cut into 12 x 20-cm rectangles. Repeat with the remaining 8 sheets of pastry.
2. Mix the cream cheese, biltong, Cheddar, spring onions and peppers together. Season with a little salt.
3. Spoon a little filling on one short end of a pastry rectangle, leaving a 1-cm space on each side. Fold the sides inwards to overlap the filling by 1 cm and then roll up to form a cylinder shape. Brush the edge of the pastry with butter to help it seal. Repeat with the remaining pastry and filling. Refrigerate for 30 minutes, or until ready to cook.
4. Brush the rolls with melted butter. Preheat the air fryer to 180 °C. Place one layer of rolls into the basket and cook for 5 minutes. Open the air fryer and turn the rolls over. Cook for a further 3-5 minutes until crisp and golden. Enjoy hot with sweet chilli sauce or chutney for dipping.

ROASTED VEGETABLE
starter PLATTER

*Create an appetising platter with roasted vegetables
and your choice of cold meats or cheeses.*

Serves: 4-6
Preparation time: 30 minutes
Air-fryer temperature: 190 °C
Cooking time: 30-33 minutes

1 medium-sized brinjal, sliced and salted
2 sweet peppers, halved and seeded
6 courgettes, trimmed and sliced lengthways
40 ml olive oil
Handful of olives (optional)
Selection of cheeses (optional)
Selection of cold meats (optional)
Sliced bread, to serve

Dressing
30 ml olive oil
10 ml red wine or sherry vinegar
1 clove garlic, crushed
30 ml fresh chopped herbs of your choice
   (basil, parsley or dill)

1. Rinse and dry the brinjal slices. Drizzle all the vegetables with olive oil. Put the peppers into the basket of the air fryer and cook for 15 minutes at 190 °C. Turn halfway through cooking.
2. Remove from the air fryer and place in a bowl. Cover with plastic wrap and set aside for 10 minutes.
3. Put the courgette slices into the basket of the air fryer and cook at 190 °C for 6 minutes. Turn halfway through cooking. Remove from the air fryer.
4. Put the brinjal slices into the basket of the air fryer. Cook for 10-12 minutes at 190 °C. Turn halfway through cooking.
5. Peel the skins from the peppers and then slice them into thick strips. Place the vegetables onto a platter.
6. Mix the dressing ingredients together and drizzle over the vegetables.
7. Add olives, meat and cheese to the platter, if you prefer, and serve with slices of crusty bread.

SAUSAGE *and* JALAPEÑO ROLLS

These home-made sausage rolls make a tasty snack. Prepare them ahead of time and then simply bake in your air fryer when you are ready to serve.

🍴 Serves: 4-6

🕐 Preparation time: 30 minutes, plus refrigeration time

🌡️ Air-fryer temperature: 200 °C

⏱️ Cooking time: 6-8 minutes per batch

300 g pork sausages
50 g (110 ml) grated Cheddar cheese
2-3 jalapeño chillies, seeded and chopped
10 ml fruit chutney
Salt, to taste
1 roll ready-made puff pastry
1 large egg, lightly beaten

1. Squeeze the meat out of the sausage casings and into a bowl. Add the Cheddar, chillies, chutney and salt.
2. Unroll the puff pastry onto a surface lightly dusted with flour and then roll it out so it is a little thinner. Brush the surface with the beaten egg. Use a sharp knife to cut into 8 x 25-cm strips.
3. Roll the meat mixture into sausage shapes and place lengthways on one half of each pastry strip, leaving a 1-cm border on the edge of the strip. Fold the pastry over to cover the filling and press the edges together with a fork to seal. Refrigerate for 10 minutes or longer.
4. Brush the tops with the beaten egg and then cut into 7-8 pieces. Preheat the air fryer to 200 °C. Put one layer of pastries into the basket and bake for 6-8 minutes until golden and cooked through. Remove from the air fryer and repeat with the remaining pastries. Enjoy warm or cold as a snack.

For a vegetarian option, replace the pork sausages with 100 g ricotta cheese and 200 g chopped roasted peppers or brinjal.

ROASTED VEGETABLE DIP
with TACO CHIPS

It takes just a few minutes to make your own crunchy taco chips in an air fryer. Make a batch and store them in an airtight container until your friends arrive. Then serve them with this healthy and delicious roasted vegetable dip.

Serves: 4-6
Preparation time: 25 minutes
Air-fryer temperature: 200 °C
Cooking time: 25-30 minutes

1 brinjal, peeled and cubed
1 red pepper, seeded and cubed
1 medium-sized red onion, roughly chopped
2 cloves garlic, chopped
1-2 ml dried crushed chillies
2 ml ground cumin
90 ml olive oil
15 ml tomato paste
15 ml red wine vinegar or lemon juice
5 ml sugar
Salt and pepper, to taste
30 ml fresh chopped coriander or basil
4-6 flour tortillas
Extra oil, for brushing
5 ml dried mixed Italian herbs or seasoned salt

1. Place the brinjal, red pepper, onion, garlic, chillies and cumin together in a bowl. Add half the olive oil and toss to coat. Put the mixture into the basket of the air fryer and cook at 200 °C for 15 minutes or until tender. Stir the vegetables halfway through the cooking time.

2. Remove from the air fryer and add the other half of the oil, the tomato paste, vinegar or lemon juice, sugar, and salt and pepper. Place in a food processor and blend until still slightly chunky. Remove from the food processor and cool, then stir in the coriander or basil.

3. **Taco chips:** Brush the flour tortillas with olive oil on both sides. Sprinkle a little of the dried herbs or seasoned salt onto one side of each tortilla. Cut into triangles. Put a layer of the pieces into the basket of the air fryer and cook at 200 °C for 3-4 minutes, giving them a toss halfway through cooking time. Once they are browned and crisp, remove from the air fryer and set aside to cool. Repeat with the remaining pieces. Serve with the dip.

CHICKEN TENDERS

You can serve these chicken tenders as a snack with a dipping sauce, or for a light lunch or supper. Top with tomato salsa in a wrap or serve with salad and chips for a meal that the kids will love.

Serves: 4-6
Preparation time: 15 minutes
Air-fryer temperature: 190 °C
Cooking time: 6-8 minutes per batch

500 g chicken breast fillets
5 ml garlic powder
5 ml onion powder
5 ml dried mixed herbs
5 ml paprika
125 ml creamy mayonnaise
Salt, to taste
250 ml panko breadcrumbs or crushed cornflakes
30 ml canola oil
Thousand Island dressing or sweet chilli sauce, to serve

1. Cut each chicken breast into 4 strips lengthways.
2. Stir the seasoning ingredients into the mayonnaise. Season with salt.
3. Dip the chicken pieces into the mayonnaise mixture to coat and then coat in the breadcrumbs or crushed cornflakes.
4. Pour the oil onto a plate and roll the chicken pieces in the oil to coat lightly, or spray with oil if you have an oil spray bottle.
5. Arrange the chicken in a single layer in the basket of the air fryer. Cook for 6-8 minutes at 190 °C until golden and cooked though. Repeat with the remaining pieces. Serve with Thousand Island dressing or sweet chilli sauce for dipping.

GARLIC BUTTER PRAWNS

Prawns are so quick and easy to prepare in an air fryer.
They make the prefect starter for a special meal.

Serves: 4

Preparation time: 5 minutes

Air-fryer temperature: 180 °C

Cooking time: approximately 10 minutes

500 g medium-sized prawns, cleaned and
   heads removed
15 ml canola oil
2 cloves garlic, crushed
35 ml melted butter
Salt and freshly ground black pepper, to taste
125 ml good-quality mayonnaise
2 ml grated lemon zest
Tabasco sauce, to taste
Lemon wedges, to serve

1. Pat the prawns dry with paper towel. Place them in a bowl and drizzle with the oil. Toss to coat.
2. Preheat the air fryer to 180 °C. Put the prawns into the basket and cook for 5 minutes at 180 °C.
3. Open the air fryer and transfer the prawns to a bowl. Mix the garlic and melted butter together. Season with salt and freshly ground black pepper. Pour over the prawns and toss to coat. Put the prawns back in the air fryer basket and cook at 200 °C for 5 minutes or until cooked through.
4. Mix the mayonnaise and lemon zest together. Add a few drops of Tabasco sauce, to taste. Serve the hot prawns with the mayonnaise and lemon wedges on the side.

CROSTINI *with* SMOKED FISH *and* TOMATO SAMBAL

Looking for a delicious and easy snack to serve your guests?
These crunchy crostini are the answer.

🍴 Serves: 6
🕐 Preparation time: 30 minutes
🌡️ Air-fryer temperature: 200 °C
⏱️ Cooking time: approximately 15 minutes

2 large ripe tomatoes, finely diced
½ medium-sized red onion, diced
10 ml sugar
15 ml grape or cider vinegar
1 chilli, seeded and chopped (optional)
10 ml freshly chopped coriander or basil
Salt and freshly ground black pepper, to taste
1 French loaf, thinly sliced
60 ml olive oil
2 cloves garlic, peeled and halved
200 g smoked snoek (or use smoked mackerel
   or trout)

1. Mix the tomatoes, onion, sugar, vinegar, chilli and coriander or basil together in a bowl. Season with salt and freshly ground black pepper. Set aside until ready to serve.
2. Brush one side of each slice of bread with olive oil. Preheat the air fryer to 200 °C and place a layer of bread slices, oiled side down, into the basket. Cook for 2-3 minutes at 200 °C until golden. Repeat with the remaining bread slices.
3. Rub the oiled side of the bread with the garlic cloves. Flake the smoked fish into small pieces, taking care to remove and discard any bones.
4. Just before serving, arrange the toasted bread slices on a platter. Top with a spoonful of the tomato sambal and a few pieces of fish. Serve immediately.

CHICKEN WINGS *with* BLUE CHEESE SAUCE

Chicken wings cook really well in an air fryer. Use your favourite spice blend, such as Portuguese or chicken spice, to flavour them or try this recipe with a creamy blue cheese dipping sauce.

Serves: 4

Preparation time: 15 minutes

Air-fryer temperature: 200 °C

Cooking time: 20-22 minutes

12 chicken wings
5 ml garlic powder
5 ml onion powder
10 ml paprika
2 ml salt
15 ml canola oil
2 spring onions, sliced

Blue cheese sauce
50 ml blue cheese
50 ml Greek yoghurt
50 ml mayonnaise
5 ml lemon juice
Tabasco sauce, to taste

1. Use a sharp knife to cut each chicken wing in half at the joint, or you can leave them whole if you prefer. Pat the pieces of chicken dry with paper towel.
2. Mix the seasoning ingredients together in a bowl. Add the chicken and toss to coat well.
3. Preheat the air fryer to 200 °C. Brush the basket of the air fryer with oil. Put the wings into the basket and cook for 20-22 minutes at 200 °C. Toss halfway through the cooking time. Remove from the air fryer and place on a serving platter. Sprinkle with spring onion slices.
4. **Sauce:** Mix the blue cheese, yoghurt, mayonnaise and lemon juice together. Add a few drops of Tabasco sauce, to taste. Serve with the wings.

SPINACH QUICHE

Quiche makes an excellent starter or light meal.
This one tastes really good served either hot or cold.

Serves: 6-8

Preparation time: 30 minutes

Air-fryer temperature: 160 °C

Cooking time: approximately 40 minutes
per batch

135 g (250 ml) cake flour
100 ml warm melted butter
100 ml grated Cheddar cheese

Filling
2 large eggs
250 ml cream (or use half milk, half cream)
20 ml cake flour
200 ml grated Cheddar cheese
Salt and pepper, to taste
100 g streaky bacon, chopped and lightly fried
250 ml cooked spinach, well drained

1. Mix the flour, melted butter and cheese together and then press into 6-8 individual tart tins. Prick the bases with a fork.

2. Preheat the air fryer to 160 °C. Place 3-4 tart tins into the basket of the air fryer and cook for 10 minutes at 160 °C. Remove from the air fryer and press the pastry up the sides of the tins if it has shrunk back a bit. Set aside to cool. Repeat with the remaining pastry bases.

3. **Filling:** Whisk the eggs, cream and flour together. Add the cheese and season with salt and pepper. Divide the bacon and spinach between the pastry bases. Pour in the cream mixture.

4. Place 3-4 quiches into the basket of the air fryer and cook for 30 minutes at 160 °C or until set and golden. Remove from the air fryer and cook the remaining quiches. If you find that the bottom of the pastry is a bit soft when you take the quiche out of the tin, you can pop it back into the air fryer for 3-5 minutes without the tin to ensure the pastry is crisp.

As a variation, replace the spinach and bacon with 50 ml chopped piquanté peppers and 100 ml feta cheese.

QUICK *and* EASY MEALS

Sticky PORK RASHERS

🍴 Serves: 4
🕐 Preparation time: 10 minutes
🌡️ Air-fryer temperature: 190 °C
⏱️ Cooking time: approximately 30 minutes

500 g pork belly rashers (about 8 mm thick)
Salt and freshly ground black pepper, to taste

Sauce
30 ml soy sauce
30 ml sweet chilli sauce
30 ml honey
15 ml canola oil
1 clove garlic, crushed
5 ml fresh ginger, grated
1 chilli, chopped (optional)

Fragrant rice, to serve
Cucumber salad or stir-fried vegetables, to serve

These sticky pork rashers are hard to resist. Cut into quarters and enjoy as a snack or starter, or serve with fragrant rice and a salad for an easy meal.

(1) Use a sharp knife or scissors to cut slits into the skin and fat on each rasher. Season with salt and freshly ground black pepper.

(2) Preheat the air fryer to 190 °C. Place the rashers into the basket in a single layer. Cook for 20 minutes at 190 °C. Turn halfway through the cooking time.

(3) Mix the sauce ingredients together until well combined. Open the air fryer and brush some of the sauce onto one side of the rashers. Cook for a further 5 minutes at 190 °C. Turn the rashers over and spread with more sauce. Cook for 5 more minutes at 190 °C until beginning to char.

(4) Remove from the air fryer and serve on a bed of rice. Spoon the remaining sauce over the rashers. Enjoy hot with cucumber salad or stir-fried vegetables on the side.

33

SALAMI *and* CHEESE BAKE

🍴 Serves: 3-4
🕐 Preparation time: 15 minutes
🌡 Air-fryer temperature: 160 °C
⏱ Cooking time: approximately 25 minutes

500 ml cubes of bread, preferably a day old
Handful of cherry tomatoes, halved
8 slices salami, sliced
160 ml grated Cheddar or mozzarella cheese
Fresh basil, plus extra to garnish
15 ml olive oil
Salt and pepper, to taste
5 large eggs
120 ml milk
50 ml grated Parmesan cheese

Made with bread and egg, this is the ideal dish to serve for breakfast or brunch. Add ham or mushrooms instead of salami if you prefer.

1. Grease a 20 x 15-cm aluminium foil container or two 10 x 7-cm containers. Put the bread, cherry tomatoes, salami, Cheddar or mozzarella and a few basil leaves into a large bowl and drizzle with olive oil. Season with salt and pepper and toss gently. Spoon into the prepared container or containers.
2. Whisk the eggs and milk together. Pour over the ingredients in the container.
3. Preheat the air fryer to 160 °C and then place the container into the basket of the air fryer. Cook for 15 minutes at 160 °C. Open the air fryer and turn the container around, then cook for a further 10 minute or until set. Remove from the air fryer and sprinkle with Parmesan and extra basil leaves.

Breakfast BUNS

🍴 Serves: 4
🕐 Preparation time: 15 minutes
🌡 Air-fryer temperature: 160 °C
⏱ Cooking time: 12-15 minutes per batch

4 crispy round buns
30 ml melted butter
410 g can baked beans in tomato sauce
Handful of cherry tomatoes, sliced
2 frankfurters or Vienna sausages, sliced
30 ml fresh sliced basil, or use 1 ml dried
4 large eggs

These crispy rolls are full of all your favourite breakfast ingredients and are a fun way to start the day.

1. Use a sharp serrated knife to cut a circle into the top of each of the buns. Scoop out the bread to form a hollow in each one. Take care not to cut through the buns.
2. Brush the outside of the buns and the inside of the hollows with the melted butter.
3. Put a spoonful of beans into each one. Top with some tomatoes, sausage slices and basil.
4. Crack an egg into a ramekin and carefully slide the egg into one of the hollows. Repeat with the remaining eggs and buns.
5. Preheat the air fryer to 160 °C. Place the buns into the basket of the air fryer. You may need to cook them in 2 batches. Bake for 12-15 minutes at 160 °C until the eggs have set. Serve hot.

TOASTED
SANDWICHES

Everybody loves a toasted sarmie and an air fryer cooks them to perfection: crisp and crunchy on the outside, and soft and gooey on the inside. Cheese, tomato and onion is the classic combo, but you can fill the toastie with your own favourite ingredients too.

🍴 Serves: 2

🕐 Preparation time: 10 minutes

🌡️ Air-fryer temperature: 180 °C

⏱️ Cooking time: approximately 8 minutes

4 slices of white bread
30 ml soft butter
125 ml grated Cheddar (or a mix of Cheddar and mozzarella)
1 tomato, sliced
½ red onion, sliced
Salt and freshly ground black pepper, to taste
10 ml fruit chutney (optional)

1. Spread the butter on one side of the bread slices. Top the unbuttered sides of 2 slices of bread with grated cheese, tomato and onion slices, and season with salt and freshly ground black pepper. Spread chutney on the unbuttered sides of the remaining slices of bread, if using, and place them on top of the filling ingredients to close the sandwiches.

2. Preheat the air fryer to 180 °C. Place the sandwiches into the basket of the air fryer. Cook for 4 minutes, then turn the sandwiches over and cook for a further 4 minutes at 180 °C. Remove from the air fryer, cut in half and enjoy hot.

For a variation, try other fillings like ham and cheese, cheese and pesto, salami and tomato or chicken mayonnaise.

PERI-PERI
STEAK

Steak cooks quickly in an air fryer but remains lovely and tender. You can use the same recipe for pork steaks or chicken breast fillets as an alternative.

🍴 Serves: 4
🕐 Preparation time: 20 minutes
🌡️ Air-fryer temperature: 200 °C
⏱️ Cooking time: 14-16 minutes

800 g rump or sirloin steak
1 onion, peeled and sliced
2 red peppers, seeded and cut into thick strips
15 ml olive oil
Ready-made peri-peri sauce (e.g. Nando's)
Chips or Portuguese rolls, to serve

1. Put the steak between two pieces of plastic wrap and hit it gently with a rolling pin to flatten it slightly if it is very thick. It should be about 1 cm thick. Cut it in half if necessary.
2. Place the onion and pepper slices together in a bowl, and drizzle with the olive oil. Toss to coat. Preheat the air fryer to 200 °C. Put the vegetables into the basket and cook for 10 minutes, tossing them halfway through the cooking time. Remove from the air fryer and set aside.
3. Pour enough sauce over the steak to coat it on both sides. Put the steak into the preheated air fryer and cook for 4-6 minutes, turning the meat halfway through the cooking time.
4. Transfer to a dish and cover with more peri-peri sauce. Wrap in aluminium foil and allow to stand for 5-10 minutes. Serve topped with the peppers and onions. Accompany with chips or serve on Portuguese rolls.

PEANUT CHICKEN
and NOODLES

Serve these chicken kebabs with an easy peanut sauce and two-minute noodles for a quick meal that's full of flavour.

Serves: 4
Preparation time: 20 minutes
Air-fryer temperature: 190 °C
Cooking time: 12-15 minutes

100 ml crunchy peanut butter
40 ml soy sauce
1 clove garlic, crushed
40 ml honey
50 ml coconut cream (optional)
4 chicken breast fillets, or use thighs, cubed
15 ml canola oil
10 ml lemon juice
1 chilli, seeded and chopped (optional)
50 ml chopped fresh coriander or mint
4 packets 2-minute noodles
Handful of salted peanuts, to serve

1. Mix the peanut butter, soy sauce, garlic, honey and coconut cream (if using) together. Spoon a quarter of the mixture over the chicken pieces and stir to coat well.
2. Thread the chicken cubes onto wooden skewers. (If your skewers are too long to fit into the air fryer basket, cut the ends off to make them a bit shorter.)
3. Preheat the air fryer to 190 °C. Place the chicken skewers into the basket of the air fryer and cook for 12-15 minutes at 190 °C, turning halfway through the cooking time. Baste with a little extra sauce when you turn the kebabs.
4. Mix the oil, lemon juice, chilli (if using) and coriander or mint together. Prepare the noodles and then drain them. Stir in the herb mixture. Top with the kebabs and sprinkle with salted peanuts. Serve with the remaining peanut sauce on the side.

FISH
and CHIPS

It only takes a few minutes to cook fish in the air fryer. Use any fish you like, but salmon trout is especially good as it is an oily fish, so it stays succulent and delicious. If you are using hake or another white fish, make sure you don't overcook it. As soon as the flesh flakes apart easily with a fork, it is done.

Serves: 4
Preparation time: 10 minutes
Air-fryer temperature: 190 °C
Cooking time: 20-22 minutes

45 ml olive oil
2 cloves garlic, crushed
15 ml lemon juice
5 ml dried oregano
1 ml each sugar, ground pepper and paprika
800 g salmon trout or other fish fillets of your choice
Oven-baked chips, to serve
Lemon wedges and mayonnaise or tartar sauce,
   to serve

(1) Mix the oil, garlic, lemon juice, oregano and other seasoning ingredients together. Spread over the fish. Set aside to marinate while you cook the chips.

(2) Preheat the air fryer to 190 °C. Cook the chips in the air fryer for 10 minutes or until crisp, tossing once halfway through the cooking time.

(3) Increase the air fryer temperature to 200 °C. Use a baking paper lining or place the fish directly into the basket. Cook for 10-12 minutes or until the fish is just cooked through. The fish is done when the flesh can be flaked apart easily with a fork.

(4) Serve the fish with chips, lemon wedges and mayonnaise or tartar sauce.

CURRIED
CHICKEN ROTI

Tender and flavoursome chicken breast wrapped in a roti...
This recipe is sure to become a family favourite. You can rather
serve the chicken with rice or salad, if you prefer.

🍴 Serves: 4

🕐 Preparation time: 20 minutes plus marinating time

🌡 Air-fryer temperature: 190 °C

⏱ Cooking time: 8-10 minutes per batch

500 g chicken breast fillets
200 ml coconut milk or Greek yoghurt
1 clove garlic, crushed
5 ml grated ginger, or use 1 ml ground ginger
30 ml butter chicken curry spice mix
15 ml tomato paste
Rotis, tomato sambal, achar and fresh coriander, to serve
Extra yoghurt, to serve (optional)

1. Use a sharp knife to cut each chicken breast fillet in half horizontally to form 2 even, flat pieces.
2. Mix the coconut milk or yoghurt, garlic, ginger, curry spice and tomato paste together. Pour over the chicken and marinate for 15 minutes or longer.
3. Preheat the air fryer to 190 °C. Line the basket of the air fryer with a piece of baking paper or brush the basket with oil. Put the chicken pieces into the basket and cook for 8-10 minutes at 190 °C or until cooked through. Turn the pieces over halfway through the cooking time. You may need to do this in two batches.
4. Remove from the air fryer and set aside for 3 minutes. Slice and serve on a roti. Top with sambal, achar, coriander and a little extra yoghurt if you like. Roll up and serve.

BARBEQUE
PORK CHOPS

*Pork chops smothered in tangy barbeque sauce
make an easy weeknight meal.*

Serves: 4
Preparation time: 15 minutes
Air-fryer temperature: 200 °C
Cooking time: 10-12 minutes

125 ml tomato sauce
30 ml red wine vinegar
30 ml Worcestershire sauce
30 ml brown sugar
5 ml mustard
4 pork chops
350 g packet of coleslaw mix
1 Granny Smith apple, grated
Vinaigrette or creamy salad dressing, to serve
Rice or baked potatoes, to serve

1. Mix the tomato sauce, vinegar, Worcestershire sauce, sugar and mustard together. Spoon over the chops and turn to coat well.
2. Preheat the air fryer to 200 °C. Line the air fryer basket with a piece of baking paper or foil. Place the chops onto the lining and cook for 10-12 minutes or until cooked through. Turn the chops over halfway through the cooking time.
3. Combine the coleslaw mix with the grated apple. Add the dressing and toss to coat. Serve the pork chops with the salad and rice or baked potatoes.

BOEREWORS
BURGERS

*Give your burger patties a surprise flavour boost
by adding boerewors to the mince.*

Serves: 4
Preparation time: 15 minutes
Air-fryer temperature: 180 °C
Cooking time: 10-12 minutes

300 g boerewors
300 g beef or pork mince
30 ml chopped parsley
Salt and freshly ground black pepper, to taste
20 ml canola oil
40 ml mayonnaise
5 ml Tabasco sauce
30 ml tomato sauce
30 ml chutney
4 hamburger buns
Toppings of your choice (sliced tomato, lettuce,
   bacon, sliced cheese, sliced onion), to serve

1. Squeeze the boerewors meat out of the sausage casing and into a bowl. Add the mince and parsley and mix to combine. Season with salt and freshly ground black pepper. Shape into 4 patties, and brush with the oil.
2. Preheat the air fryer to 180 °C. Place the patties into the basket of the air fryer and cook for 10-12 minutes, turning halfway through the cooking time.
3. Mix the mayonnaise, Tabasco, tomato sauce and chutney together. Spread onto the buns. Top with the burger patties and the topping ingredients of your choice.

MEATY SALSA
TACOS

A definite weeknight winner, this meaty treat is very easy to prepare and it tastes so good that everyone will be asking for seconds.

Serves: 4

Preparation time: 15 minutes

Air-fryer temperature: 200 °C

Cooking time: approximately 10 minutes

500 g pork fillet (or use ostrich fillet or chicken breast fillet)
20 ml canola oil
20 ml Mexican spice mix (you can also use steak seasoning or barbeque seasoning)
2 ripe avocados, mashed
1 tomato, chopped
¼ red onion, finely chopped
30 ml chopped fresh coriander
5 ml lemon juice
Salt, to taste
400 g jar Mexican salsa
156 g box corn tacos
Shredded lettuce, to serve

1. Cut the meat into 2-cm cubes. Place the cubes into a bowl and add the oil and the spice mix. Toss to coat well.
2. Preheat the air fryer to 200 °C. Put the meat into the basket of the air fryer and cook for 6-8 minutes until the meat is cooked through and browned. Toss halfway through the cooking time.
3. Mix the avocado, tomato, onion, coriander and lemon juice together. Season with salt.
4. Heat the tacos in the air fryer at 180 °C for 2 minutes, or until golden. Fill the tacos with the meat, then add the salsa, avocado mixture and lettuce, and enjoy.

FAMILY *meals*

TANDOORI CHICKEN

🍴 Serves: 4

🕐 Preparation time: 15 minutes,
   plus marinating time

🌡️ Air-fryer temperature: 180 °C

⏱️ Cooking time: approximately 25 minutes

150 ml full-cream plain yoghurt
30-45 ml tandoori spice mix
15 ml lemon juice
1 clove garlic, crushed
5 ml grated fresh ginger (or 1 ml ground ginger)
4 chicken thighs and 4 legs
Naan bread or rice and salad, to serve

Chicken portions are marinated in a spicy yoghurt marinade that ensures tender and tasty results.

1. Mix the yoghurt, tandoori spice, lemon juice, garlic and ginger together. Spread over the chicken pieces so they are well coated. Set aside to marinate for 30 minutes or longer.
2. Preheat the air fryer to 180 °C. Place a baking paper lining into the air fryer basket, if you prefer, otherwise put the chicken pieces directly into the basket.
3. Cook the chicken for 20-25 minutes, turning the pieces over halfway through the cooking time. To check if the chicken is done, the juices should run clear when you cut into the meat.
4. Serve hot with naan bread or rice and a salad.

LAMB CHOPS *with*
MINTY COURGETTES

Lamb chops cook very well in an air fryer. They are delicious served with this easy-to-prepare courgette side dish.

Serves: 4

Preparation time: 20 minutes, plus marinating time

Air-fryer temperature: 200 °C

Cooking time: approximately 25 minutes

2 cloves garlic, crushed
5 ml grated lemon zest
20 ml lemon juice
5 ml dried mint
40 ml olive oil
Salt and freshly ground black pepper, to taste
8 lamb loin or chump chops
250 g courgettes, sliced
125 ml crumbled feta cheese
Pita breads or pasta rice, to serve

1. Mix together the garlic, lemon zest, lemon juice, 2 ml dried mint, 15 ml olive oil and salt and freshly ground black pepper. Rub over the chops and allow to marinate for 30 minutes or longer.
2. Drizzle the remaining oil over the courgettes and add the remaining dried mint. Toss to coat.
3. Preheat the air fryer to 200 °C.
4. Place the courgettes into the air fryer basket and cook for 15 minutes, tossing halfway through the cooking time. Remove from the air fryer and set aside.
5. Place the chops into the basket of the air fryer and cook for 8-10 minutes. Turn over halfway through cooking. Set aside to rest for 3 minutes.
6. Add the feta to the courgettes. Serve with the chops accompanied by pita bread or pasta rice.

CURRY MINCE
PIES

Treat the family to a home-made pie. Use ready-made puff pastry and fill with this Cape Malay-style curried mince, or use leftover meat stew or savoury mince as a filling instead.

Serves: 4
Preparation time: 40 minutes
Air-fryer temperature: 190 °C
Cooking time: approximately 50 minutes

20 ml canola oil
1 medium onion, finely chopped
1 clove garlic, crushed
5 ml grated ginger
1 cinnamon stick
10-15 ml medium-strength curry powder
3 ml each ground cumin and coriander
1 ml ground turmeric
300 g lean beef mince
1 tomato, grated
1 medium-sized potato, peeled and diced
1 beef stock cube
50 ml frozen peas
1 roll ready-made puff pastry
1 large egg, lightly beaten

1. Heat the oil in a frying pan and sauté the onion until soft. Add the garlic, ginger and cinnamon stick and cook for 2 minutes. Add the ground spices and cook for a further minute.
2. Increase the heat and add the mince. Stir until the meat is lightly browned. Add the tomato and the potato. Reduce the heat and cover the saucepan. Cook for 15 minutes.
3. Dissolve the stock cube in 30 ml of boiling water. Add to the mince mixture along with the peas. Cook for a further 15 minutes and season to taste. Remove from the heat and cool completely.
4. Unroll the pastry onto a lightly floured surface. Cut 15-cm circles out of the pastry.
5. Place a large spoonful of the mince mixture onto each circle of pastry. Brush the edges of the pastry with the beaten egg. Fold the pastry over the filling and press the edges together to seal. Make a hole in the top of each pie.
6. Preheat the air fryer to 180 °C. Brush the pies with the beaten egg and place 2 or 3 pies into the air fryer basket. Bake for 15 minutes or until crisp and golden.

TOMATO *and herb*
CRUMBED FISH

Use hake or other white fish to prepare this dish. It's a healthy choice and has a wonderful Mediterranean flavour.

Serves: 4

Preparation time: 15 minutes, plus marinating time

Air-fryer temperature: 200 °C

Cooking time: approximately 10 minutes

500 g white fish fillets
2 cloves garlic, crushed
10 ml lemon juice
30 ml tomato paste
5 ml dried oregano
Salt, to taste
125 ml toasted breadcrumbs
30 ml sunflower oil
Pasta salad or green salad, to serve

1. Cut the fish into large chunks and pat dry.
2. Mix the garlic, lemon juice, tomato paste and oregano together. Season with salt. Add to the fish and stir to coat the pieces. Marinate for 30 minutes.
3. Spread the breadcrumbs out on a plate and roll the pieces of fish in the breadcrumbs. Brush or drizzle with oil.
4. Preheat the air fryer to 200 °C and bake for 10 minutes. Turn the pieces over halfway through the cooking time. Cook until golden and cooked through. Serve with pasta salad or green salad.

Pasta salad

Mix 300 g cooked pasta noodles with 50 ml basil pesto, 30 ml olive oil, 125 ml diced sweet peppers and 2 diced tomatoes.

MASALA
FISH

A quick, spicy fish dish that's full of flavour and easy to prepare.

 Serves: 4

Preparation time: 15 minutes

Air-fryer temperature: 200 °C

Cooking time: 8-10 minutes

5 ml cumin seeds
7 ml ground cumin
3 ml ground turmeric
2 cloves garlic, crushed
1-2 fresh chillies, seeded and chopped
50 ml canola oil
Salt, to taste
500 g white fish steaks (skinned and filleted)
2 tomatoes, cut into thick slices
Rice and vegetables, to serve
Fresh coriander, to garnish

1. Mix the spices, garlic, chillies and oil together. Season with salt.
2. Cut 2-3 diagonal slits into each piece of fish. Spread the spice mixture over each piece of fish and into the slits.
3. Preheat the air fryer to 200 °C. Place a piece of baking paper in the bottom of the air fryer basket as a lining if you prefer, or place the ingredients directly into the basket. Place the tomato slices underneath the pieces of fish. Cook for 8-10 minutes or until the fish is cooked through.
4. Serve hot accompanied by rice and vegetables and garnish with coriander.

MUSTARD-BAKED
PORK SCHNITZEL

This versatile recipe can be prepared using thin slices of pork or beef, or use flattened pieces of chicken breast fillet. Crush cornflakes in a food processor or put them into a sealable bag and crush them with a rolling pin. They make a tasty and crunchy coating.

Serves: 4

Preparation time: 20 minutes

Air-fryer temperature: 200 °C

Cooking time: 10-12 minutes

60 ml sour cream
25 ml Dijon mustard, plus extra to serve
5 ml mustard seeds
4 pieces of pork schnitzel
250 ml cornflake crumbs (or use toasted breadcrumbs)
Salad and potatoes, to serve

1. Mix the sour cream, mustard and mustard seeds together. Spread the mixture over the meat, then press each piece into the cornflake crumbs to coat on both sides.
2. Preheat the air fryer to 200 °C. Place the pork pieces into the basket of the air fryer and cook for 10-12 minutes or until cooked through and golden. Turn the pieces over halfway through the cooking time.
3. Serve with extra mustard on the side along with a salad and roast potato slices.

Roast potato slices

Peel 4 boiled potatoes and cut into thick slices. Drizzle with olive oil and sprinkle with seasoning salt or barbeque spice. Preheat the air fryer to 200 °C and cook the potato slices for 10 minutes, turning halfway through the cooking time.

CHUTNEY CHICKEN
with COUSCOUS

An old favourite that can be cooked easily in an air fryer. Serve with colourful peppers and couscous.

Serves: 4

Preparation time: 30 minutes

Air-fryer temperature: 180 °C

Cooking time: approximately 45 minutes

30 ml olive oil
Salt and freshly ground black pepper, to taste
1 red and 1 yellow pepper, seeded and sliced
1 red onion, halved and sliced lengthways
6-8 chicken thighs or mix of legs and thighs
45 ml cornflour
125 ml fruit chutney
125 ml mayonnaise
15 ml white wine vinegar
10 ml Dijon mustard
10 ml soy sauce
250 ml prepared chicken stock
250 ml couscous (use regular or pearl couscous)
50 ml fresh chopped parsley or coriander

1. Preheat the air fryer to 180 °C. Drizzle half the oil over the peppers and onion and then place into the basket of the air fryer. Cook for 10 minutes, tossing halfway through the cooking time. Once cooked, remove from the air fryer and set aside.

2. Drizzle the remaining oil over the chicken pieces. Rub to coat and season with salt and freshly ground black pepper. Sprinkle with cornflour so that the pieces are all coated.

3. Place the pieces of chicken into the basket of the air fryer and cook for 15 minutes. Turn the pieces over halfway through the cooking time.

4. Meanwhile, mix the chutney, mayonnaise, vinegar, mustard and soy sauce together in a bowl. Remove the chicken pieces from the air fryer and toss in the mixture to coat.

5. Place a baking paper lining into the air fryer basket if you prefer, or place the chicken pieces directly into the basket. Cook for 15-20 minutes at 180 °C, turning the pieces over and spooning any leftover chutney sauce over the pieces halfway through the cooking time. To check if the chicken is done, the juices should run clear when the meat is cut open.

6. **Couscous**: Pour the hot stock over the couscous and cover with a lid. Leave to soak. Once you are ready to serve, stir in the cooked peppers and onion and the herbs. Serve with the chicken.

BACON-WRAPPED
MEATLOAF

A family favourite that can be prepared ahead of time and then baked just before dinner.

🍴 Serves: 4

🕐 Preparation time: 20 minutes

🌡️ Air-fryer temperature: 160 °C

⏱️ Cooking time: 35-40 minutes

1 large egg
2 slices of bread, crusts removed
30 ml olive oil
50 ml freshly chopped parsley
2 cloves garlic, crushed
2 ml dried thyme
400 g lean beef mince or half pork and half beef mince
15 ml mustard powder
5 ml paprika
10 ml Bovril
Salt and freshly ground black pepper, to taste
200 g streaky bacon
Sweet potato slices or mashed potato and salad, to serve

1. Put the egg into a bowl and whisk lightly. Add the bread and allow to soak.
2. Break up the soaked bread with a fork, then add all the remaining ingredients except the bacon. Season with salt and freshly ground black pepper and mix well.
3. Shape into a roll. Wrap the bacon around the mince roll, and place in a greased aluminium 9 x 20-cm loaf tin.
4. Preheat the air fryer to 160 °C. Place the meatloaf into the basket of the air fryer and cook for 35-40 minutes or until cooked through.
5. Remove from the air fryer and allow to rest for 5 minutes before turning out onto a platter and slicing. Serve hot with roasted sweet potato slices or mashed potato and salad.

Roasted sweet potato slices

Peel 1-2 orange sweet potatoes and cut into slices. Soak them in a bowl of cold water for 30 minutes. Drain well and pat dry. Drizzle with olive oil and season to taste. Preheat the air fryer to 180 °C and cook for 10-12 minutes, turning the pieces over halfway through the cooking time.

STUFFED
OSTRICH STEAKS

Tender ostrich fillets with a surprise filling in the centre; you must give them a try!

🍴 Serves: 3-4

🕐 Preparation time: 30 minutes, plus marinating time

🌡️ Air-fryer temperature: 200 °C

⏱️ Cooking time: 15-20 minutes

40 ml balsamic vinegar
40 ml soy sauce
25 ml olive oil
7 ml brown sugar
2,5 ml dried mixed herbs
5 ml Dijon mustard
800 g ostrich fillet, cut into 3-4 portions
125 ml cream cheese
1 clove garlic, crushed
1-2 jalapeño chillies, seeded and chopped
Potato wedges and roasted vegetables, to serve

1. Mix the balsamic vinegar, soy sauce, oil, sugar, herbs and mustard together in a bowl. Add the meat pieces and turn to coat well. Set aside to marinate for 1 hour or longer.

2. Mix the cream cheese, garlic and jalapeño chillies together.

3. Cut a slit into the middle of the steaks and stuff with the cream cheese filling. Secure the opening closed, using a toothpick. Tie a piece of string around each piece of meat to create a neat, secure shape.

4. Preheat the air fryer to 200 °C. Place the steaks into the basket of the air fryer and cook for 5 minutes. Open the air fryer and turn the steaks over. Cook for a further 5-10 minutes depending on how you like your steak done. Remove from the air fryer, cover loosely with aluminium foil and set aside to rest for 10 minutes. Remove the string and toothpicks and serve hot with potato wedges and roasted vegetables.

Potato wedges

Use floury potatoes that are good for making chips. Cut 3-4 potatoes into wedges. Soak in cold water for 30 minutes. Drain and pat dry. Drizzle with a little oil and toss to coat. Preheat the air fryer to 160 °C and cook the wedges for 12 minutes. Toss the wedges and then increase the heat to 180 °C and cook for a further 12-15 minutes or until golden and cooked through.

PORK BELLY ROAST
with PEARS AND FENNEL

When you need something special that doesn't require much effort, this is the answer. The meat is soft and succulent and the crunchy crackling is the best.

🍴 Serves: 4
🕐 Preparation time: 30 minutes
🌡️ Air-fryer temperature: 190 °C
⏱️ Cooking time: 1 hour, 25 minutes

1,5 kg piece of pork belly (ask the butcher to
   score the skin)
30 ml coarse salt
30 ml canola oil
15 ml fennel seeds
10 ml cumin seeds
10 ml barbeque spice
30 ml brown sugar
1 fresh fennel bulb, sliced
2 firm but ripe pears, cored and cut into wedges
30 ml butter

1. Use a sharp knife to score the bottom side of the pork belly. Cover the skin with the coarse salt and set aside for 30 minutes. Wipe off the salt and any moisture with paper towel.
2. Rub the piece of meat with oil on both sides. Crush the fennel and cumin seeds in a pestle and mortar. Remove 5 ml of the spice mix and set aside. Add the barbeque spice to the remaining spice mix. Rub over the bottom side of the meat.
3. Preheat the air fryer to 190 °C. Place a piece of aluminium foil into the basket of the air fryer for the meat to rest on. Place the meat into the air fryer, skin side up and cook for 45 minutes.
4. Remove the meat from the air fryer and sprinkle half of the sugar over the bottom of the meat. Return to the air fryer, skin side up, and cook at 190 °C for a further 15-20 minutes or until the crackling is crisp and golden. Remove from the air fryer and set aside.
5. Place the fennel bulb and pears into an aluminium container or ovenproof dish. Add the 5 ml of spice that was set aside and then dot with butter and sprinkle with the remaining sugar. Place into the basket of the air fryer and cook at 180 °C for 15-20 minutes or until the ingredients are tender. Toss halfway through the cooking time.
6. Use a sharp serrated knife to cut the pork into slices. Serve with the pears and fennel.

JUICY
ROAST CHICKEN

Sunday lunch is made easy with this succulent chicken roasted whole in the air fryer.

Serves: 4

Preparation time: 15 minutes

Air-fryer temperature: 160 °C

Cooking time: 50 minutes

50 ml soft butter
30 ml Dijon mustard
10 ml fresh chopped thyme or lemon thyme
1 ml salt
1,250 kg whole chicken
1 onion, peeled and cut into wedges
Roasted baby potatoes and vegetables, to serve

1. Mix the butter, mustard, thyme and salt together.
2. Carefully put your fingers underneath the chicken skin, between the flesh and the skin, and lift the skin up to create a pocket. Spread the butter mixture into the pocket so it forms a layer between the skin and the flesh.
3. Put the onion wedges into the chicken cavity and tie the legs closed with a piece of string.
4. Preheat the air fryer to 160 °C. Place the chicken, breast side down, into the air fryer basket and cook for 20 minutes. Open the air fryer and turn the chicken over carefully. Close and cook for a further 20-30 minutes until the chicken is done and the juices run clear when the meat is cut with a sharp knife. The chicken should be 85 °C if tested with a meat thermometer.
5. Remove from the air fryer and set aside to rest for 10 minutes. Remove the onion from the cavity. Carve and serve the chicken with roasted baby potatoes and vegetables of your choice.

Roasted baby potatoes

Drizzle a little olive oil over washed baby potatoes. Preheat the air fryer to 190 °C and cook the potatoes for 12-15 minutes, tossing halfway through the cooking time.

VEGETABLES
and
SIDE DISHES

Cinnamon ROASTED PUMPKIN

🍴 Serves: 4

🕐 Preparation time: 10 minutes

🌡️ Air-fryer temperature: 180 °C

⏱️ Cooking time: 30 minutes

500 g pumpkin slices or cubes
5 ml grated orange zest
50 ml brown sugar
5 ml ground cinnamon
2 star anise
50 ml butter, melted

You can't go wrong with South Africa's favourite combination of pumpkin and cinnamon. A perfect side dish for most meals.

1. Put the pumpkin pieces into a bowl. Add the remaining ingredients and toss to coat.
2. Transfer to a greased aluminium baking dish or an ovenproof dish.
3. Preheat the air fryer to 180 °C. Put the dish into the basket of the air fryer and cook for 30 minutes or until tender. Stir halfway through the cooking time.

Stuffed MUSHROOMS

Serves: 4-6
Preparation time: 15 minutes
Air-fryer temperature: 200 °C
Cooking time: 15-20 minutes

400 g medium-sized brown mushrooms, stalks removed
30 ml olive oil
1 clove garlic, crushed
30 ml melted butter
125 ml toasted breadcrumbs or panko breadcrumbs
1 ml dried crushed chillies (optional)
Salt and freshly ground black pepper, to taste
½ x 400 g can tomato and onion braai relish
125 ml grated Cheddar cheese

Stuffed mushrooms make a great starter or side dish. They are also a good vegetarian option.

1. Brush the mushrooms with olive oil. Preheat the air fryer to 200 °C. Put the mushrooms, stem side down, into the air fryer basket and cook for 5 minutes.
2. Mix the garlic with the melted butter. Stir into the breadcrumbs and add chillies (if using). Season with salt and freshly ground black pepper.
3. Remove the mushrooms from the air fryer, turn them stem side up and then fill each one with a spoonful of the braai relish and grated cheese. Top with the breadcrumb mixture. Drizzle with a little extra olive oil and put the mushrooms carefully back into the basket of the air fryer.
4. Cook for 10-15 minutes at 200 °C until the mushrooms are tender and the crumbs are golden.

Roasted CAULIFLOWER

Serves: 4
Preparation time: 10 minutes
Air-fryer temperature: 190 °C
Cooking time: 12-15 minutes

500 g cauliflower
50 ml olive oil
1 clove garlic, crushed
50 ml grated Parmesan cheese
2 ml ground paprika
5 ml fresh chopped thyme, or use 1 ml dried
Salt and freshly ground black pepper, to taste

A good side dish to serve with roast meat or chicken.

1. Break or cut the cauliflower into florets and place them in a bowl.
2. Mix the remaining ingredients together. Add to the cauliflower and toss well to coat. Season with salt and freshly ground black pepper.
3. Preheat the air fryer to 190 °C. Put the cauliflower into the basket of the air fryer and cook for 12-15 minutes or until browned and tender. Toss halfway through the cooking time.

SWEETCORN
SALAD

Colourful and fresh, this salad is perfect to serve as a side dish at a braai or when entertaining.

Serves: 4
Preparation time: 30 minutes
Air-fryer temperature: 200 °C
Cooking time: approximately 15 minutes

2-3 thick slices of ciabatta bread or other white bread, cubed
80 ml olive oil
Salt, to taste
2-3 corn on the cob
1 clove garlic, crushed
60 ml olive oil
30 ml red wine vinegar
1 punnet cherry tomatoes, halved
1 small red onion, sliced
10 black olives, pitted and halved
Handful of fresh parsley or basil, torn

1. Put the bread cubes into a bowl and drizzle with 10 ml olive oil. Add salt to taste. Toss well to coat the cubes.
2. Preheat the air fryer to 200 °C. Put the bread into the basket of the air fryer and cook for 5 minutes or until crisp. Toss halfway through the cooking time. Remove from the air fryer and set aside.
3. Rub the sweetcorn with 10 ml olive oil. Put the corn into the basket of the air fryer and cook for 10-12 minutes until tender, turning the sweetcorn halfway through the cooking time. Remove from the air fryer and set aside to cool.
4. Mix the garlic, remaining olive oil and vinegar together. Slice the corn off the cob and add the remaining salad ingredients. Add the dressing and mix gently to coat. Season with salt and freshly ground black pepper.

MOROCCAN-SPICED
BUTTERNUT *and*
NAARTJIE SALAD

Serve as a side salad or add cooked chicken or chickpeas and enjoy as a light main course.

Serves: 4

Preparation time: 25 minutes

Air-fryer temperate: 180 °C

Cooking time: approximately 30 minutes

1 medium butternut, peeled and cubed
  (or use a packet of ready-cubed butternut)
30 ml olive oil
20 ml Moroccan spice blend/rub
3 baby gem lettuces, broken into leaves
30 g wild rocket
2 naartjies, peeled and segmented
½ red onion, thinly sliced
50 ml toasted pumpkin seeds
50 ml crumbled blue or feta cheese
Olive oil and balsamic vinegar, to serve

1. Place the butternut in a bowl. Drizzle with olive oil and sprinkle with the Moroccan spices. Toss to coat. Preheat the air fryer to 180 °C. Place the butternut into the basket of the air fryer. Cook for 25-30 minutes or until tender and slightly charred. Turn the pieces over halfway through the cooking time.

2. Remove from the air fryer and set aside to cool. Place the lettuce, rocket, naartjie segments and onion slices onto a platter and top with the cooked butternut. Sprinkle with pumpkin seeds and blue cheese or feta, and drizzle with olive oil and balsamic vinegar.

Pap TART

🍴 Serves: 6
🕐 Preparation time: 20 minutes
🌡️ Air-fryer temperature: 180 °C
⏱️ Cooking time: approximately 30 minutes

650 ml warm water or prepared vegetable stock
150 g quick-cook mealie meal
15 ml butter
2 ml salt
½ x 410 g can creamed sweetcorn
1 x 410 g can chopped Italian or
    Indian-flavoured tomatoes
250 ml grated Cheddar cheese

Always a favourite at the braai, pap tart bakes quickly in the air fryer.

1. Pour 400 ml water or stock into a saucepan. Mix the mealie meal with the remaining water or stock. Add to the saucepan and stir well. Add the butter and salt.
2. Cook over a medium heat on the stove until thickened, stirring occasionally. Stir in the creamed sweetcorn.
3. Grease a 15 x 20-cm aluminium baking container or ovenproof dish. Spoon a layer of the cooked *pap* into the container. Spread a layer of tomato and half the cheese over the *pap*.
4. Repeat the layers, ending off with cheese.
5. Preheat the air fryer to 180 °C. Place the container into the basket of the air fryer and bake for 20 minutes until the cheese is melted and golden. Enjoy as a side dish.

Mealie-pap CHIPS

🍴 Serves: 4-6
🕐 Preparation time: 20 minutes, plus cooling time
🌡️ Air-fryer temperature: 200 °C
⏱️ Cooking time: approximately 30 minutes

650 ml prepared chicken or vegetable stock
150 g quick-cook mealie meal, plus 30 ml extra
40 g Parmesan cheese, grated
10 ml dried mixed herbs
1 ml garlic powder
50 ml canola oil

Change things up a bit and serve these mealie-pap chips instead of potatoes as an interesting side dish. They also make a really moreish snack when served with chakalaka as a dipping sauce.

1. Bring 400 ml stock to the boil in a saucepan. Mix the mealie meal with the remaining stock. Add this mixture to the stock in the saucepan, stirring constantly. Cook over a medium heat until thickened.
2. Add the cheese, herbs and garlic powder, and stir to combine. Pour into a greased and lined 20-cm square tin and refrigerate for 1 hour until firm.
3. Cut the chilled mealie *pap* into chips and brush on all sides with canola oil. Dust with the extra mealie meal.
4. Spray with oil if you have an oil sprayer bottle or brush with a little extra oil. Preheat the air fryer to 200 °C and place the chips into the air fryer basket. Cook for 15-20 minutes until crisp on the edges. Turn the chips halfway through cooking.

Roasted PEPPERS

🍴 Serves: 4
🕐 Preparation time: 5 minutes
🌡️ Air-fryer temperature: 190 °C
⏱️ Cooking time: 5-8 minutes

6 baby sweet peppers, halved and seeded
1-3 jalapeño peppers, seeded and cut into quarters
  (optional)
15 ml olive oil

Brighten up your dinner plate with a helping of sweet roasted peppers. They are ready in minutes.

1. Put all the peppers into a bowl and drizzle with the oil. Toss to coat.
2. Preheat the air fryer to 190 °C. Put the peppers into the basket and cook for 5-8 minutes or until tender, tossing halfway through the cooking time.

Potato CAKES

🍴 Serves: 4
🕐 Preparation time: 20 minutes
🌡️ Air-fryer temperature: 200 °C
⏱️ Cooking time: approximately 20 minutes

4 medium- to large-sized potatoes, boiled and cooled
5 ml barbeque seasoning or seasoning mix of
  your choice
Salt and freshly ground black pepper, to taste
1 large egg, whisked
20 ml canola oil

Serve these potato cakes as a side dish with roast meat or sausages and gravy, or top with a fried egg as a light lunch with a salad.

1. Peel the potatoes and grate them into a bowl. Add the seasoning spice along with salt and freshly ground black pepper.
2. Stir in the egg, then shape the mixture into 4 patties.
3. Pour the oil onto a plate and dip both sides of the patties into the oil, or spray with oil if you have an oil spray bottle.
4. Preheat the air fryer to 200 °C. Put the potato cakes into the basket of the air fryer. Cook for 20 minutes or until crisp and golden.

ROASTED BABY CARROTS
and PINEAPPLE

Pineapple roasted in an air fryer is packed with sweet and juicy flavour. It combines well with carrots to create this pretty side dish.

Serves: 4
Preparation time: 10 minutes
Air-fryer temperature: 180 °C
Cooking time: 25-30 minutes

1 bunch baby carrots, peeled and trimmed
1 pineapple, peeled and sliced
3 ml grated ginger
50 ml prepared vegetable stock or water
15 ml honey
30 ml butter
Cayenne pepper, to taste
Salt, to taste

1. Cut the carrots in half lengthways. Put the carrots and pineapple into a 15 x 20-cm aluminium container or ovenproof dish.
2. Mix the ginger, stock, honey and butter together and add a little cayenne pepper and salt. Pour over the carrots and pineapple.
3. Preheat the air fryer to 180 °C. Place the container into the basket of the air fryer and cook for 25-30 minutes until the carrots are just tender. Toss halfway through the cooking time.
4. Serve hot as an accompaniment to chicken or pork. It's also excellent served with curries.

LOCAL
favourites

MEALIE BREAD
with biltong

¶¶ Makes: 1 large loaf or 2 smaller loaves

🕐 Preparation time: 15 minutes

🌡 Air-fryer temperature: 160 °C

⏱ Cooking time: 30 minutes

330 g sweetcorn kernels
120 ml milk
125 ml chopped, thinly sliced, soft beef biltong
2 large eggs, lightly beaten
30 ml melted butter
180 g (330 ml) white bread flour
30 ml mealie meal
15 ml sugar
15 ml baking powder
5 ml salt
2 ml paprika
15 ml extra melted butter, for brushing

Serve sliced and spread with butter while it's still warm. Ideal as a snack at a braai or while you're watching the rugby.

1 Grease a 15 x 20-cm rectangular aluminium tin. Blend 250 ml of the corn with the milk in a food processor until smooth. Pour into a bowl and add the remaining corn, biltong, eggs and melted butter.

2 Stir in the flour, mealie meal, sugar, baking powder, salt and paprika. Pour into the prepared tin.

3 Preheat the air fryer to 160 °C. Place the tin into the basket of the air fryer and cook for 30 minutes. A skewer inserted should come out clean when done. Remove from the air fryer and brush with extra melted butter.

4 Set aside to cool in the tin for 20 minutes before inverting onto a cooling rack. Serve warm, spread with butter.

SOSATIES

The combination of sweet-and-sour fruity flavours with a touch of curry is something we love in South Africa. Sosaties are always popular and you can use your favourite meat or chicken to prepare them.

🍴 Serves: 4- 6

🕐 Preparation time: 35 minutes,
   plus marinating time

🌡 Air-fryer temperature: 200 °C

⏱ Cooking time: approximately 10 minutes
   per batch

Marinade
25 ml canola oil
½ onion, finely chopped
5 ml grated ginger
2 cloves garlic, crushed
25 ml curry powder
5 ml each ground cumin and coriander
10 ml brown sugar
5 ml cornflour
60 ml apricot jam
60 ml white wine vinegar
60 ml dry white wine
Salt and freshly ground black pepper, to taste

Sosaties
800 g lamb leg meat, or use beef, ostrich, pork or
   chicken thigh fillets
80 g soft dried apricots
1 red onion, cut into wedges
200 g streaky bacon, cut into 2-cm pieces (optional)

1. **Marinade:** Heat the oil in a small saucepan. Add the onion and sauté until soft. Add the ginger, garlic and spices and sauté for a few minutes. Add the remaining marinade ingredients and bring to the boil. Reduce the heat and simmer for 5 minutes, stirring occasionally. Remove from the heat and cool completely. Season with salt and freshly ground black pepper.

2. Cut the meat into cubes and place in a glass bowl. Pour the cooled marinade over the meat and stir to coat well. Cover and set aside to marinate for a few hours or overnight in the fridge (bring back to room temperature before cooking).

3. Thread the meat onto wooden skewers alternating with pieces of apricot, onions and bacon (if using). Trim the skewers if necessary to fit into the air fryer.

4. Preheat the air fryer to 200 °C. Place a layer of sosaties into the basket of the air fryer and cook for 10 minutes, turning the sosaties halfway through cooking time. You may need to do this in two batches. Serve hot with rice and salads.

BOEREWORS *with*
CHERRY TOMATO RELISH

If you don't want to braai, but have a craving for a boerie roll, cook it in the air fryer.

🍴 Serves: 4

🕐 Preparation time: 15 minutes

🌡 Air-fryer temperature: 200 °C

⏱ Cooking time: approximately 20 minutes

Tomato relish

250 g baby tomatoes, halved
1 onion, sliced
1 clove garlic, crushed
2 ml sugar
1 chilli, seeded and sliced (optional)
5 ml paprika
20 ml olive oil
Salt and freshly ground black pepper, to taste
5 ml red wine vinegar

Boerie rolls

500 g boerewors
4 hot dog rolls, to serve

1. **Tomato relish**: Place all of the relish ingredients, except for the vinegar, into a bowl. Toss to coat. Season with salt and freshly ground black pepper.

2. Place the mixture into an aluminium container or ovenproof dish. Preheat the air fryer to 200 °C. Place the roasting dish into the basket of the air fryer and cook for 10 minutes. Stop and stir the mixture halfway through the cooking time. Once the ingredients are soft, they are done. Remove from the air fryer and add the vinegar.

3. Prick the boerewors a few times with a kebab stick. Place the boerewors in the basket of the air fryer and cook for 8-10 minutes at 200 °C. Turn the boerewors over halfway through the **cooking time**. Cook until the boerewors is browned **and** breaks easily.

4. Serve the boerewors on a roll **topped with** the tomato relish.

STEAK
GATSBY

Tuck into this home-made version
of the popular take-away treat.

Serves: 4

Preparation time: 20 minutes,
  plus marinating time

Air-fryer temperature: 200 °C

Cooking time: approximately 25 minutes

800 g minute steaks
5 ml ground turmeric
30 ml leaf masala
5 ml paprika
10 ml barbeque spice
4 cloves garlic, crushed
15 ml grated ginger
15 ml brown vinegar, plus extra for drizzling
5 ml sugar
60 ml canola oil
2 onions, sliced
750 g oven-baked chips
1 large French loaf, cut in half lengthways
Sliced tomato, lettuce, coriander, chilli sauce
  (optional), to serve

1. Place the pieces of meat between two sheets of plastic wrap and hit gently with a rolling pin or meat mallet to flatten.
2. Mix the spices, garlic, ginger, vinegar, sugar and 30 ml oil together and spread over the meat. Set aside to marinate at room temperature for 1 hour.
3. Put the onion slices into a bowl and add the remaining oil. Toss well to coat.
4. Preheat the air fryer to 200 °C. Put the onions into the basket of the air fryer and cook for 8 minutes. Stir halfway through the cooking time. The onions should be slightly charred when they are done. Remove from the air fryer and set aside.
5. Reduce the heat to 190 °C and cook the oven-baked chips for 10 minutes until done. Toss once during cooking. Set aside. Drizzle with brown vinegar and season to taste.
6. Increase the air fryer temperature to 200 °C and add the steak to the basket. Cook for 3-5 minutes, turning halfway through the cooking time.
7. To serve, spread the bread with butter. Top with tomato, lettuce, coriander, chips, steak and onions. Add some chilli sauce, if you like. Wrap tightly in foil and allow to stand for 5-10 minutes so the flavours can mingle. Cut into pieces and enjoy.

BOBOTIE

Possibly our favourite local speciality, bobotie is always a winner.

Serves: 4-6

Preparation time: 30 minutes

Air-fryer temperature: 160 °C

Cooking time: approximately 35 minutes

15 ml canola oil
1 onion, finely chopped
15 ml medium-strength curry powder
1 ml ground turmeric
500 g lean beef mince
1 slice of bread
60 ml milk
1 small green apple, peeled and grated
30 ml fruit chutney
15 ml white wine vinegar
Handful of sultanas (optional)
Salt and freshly ground black pepper, to taste
4-6 bay leaves
1 large egg
120 ml milk
Yellow rice, fruit chutney and salad, to serve

1. Heat the oil in a frying pan on the stove and add the onion. Cook over a low heat until the onion is soft. Add the curry powder and turmeric and cook for a minute. Increase the heat and add the mince. Cook for a few minutes, stirring occasionally, until the mince has browned lightly.

2. Soak the bread in the 60 ml milk. Once it is soft, mix it into the mince. Add the apple, chutney, vinegar and sultanas (if using). Season well with salt and freshly ground black pepper.

3. Spoon the mixture into a 15 x 20-cm greased aluminium baking tin or ovenproof dish. Press the bay leaves into the mince mixture. Whisk the egg with 120 ml milk and pour over the mince mixture.

4. Preheat the air fryer to 160 °C. Put the baking tin into the basket of the air fryer and cook for 25-30 minutes until golden and set. Serve hot with rice, chutney and salad.

SNOEK *with*
APRICOT GLAZE

*Use fresh or frozen snoek to prepare
this traditional South African fish dish.*

🍴 Serves: 4

🕐 Preparation time: 15 minutes,
 plus standing time

🌡️ Air-fryer temperature: 190 °C

⏱️ Cooking time: approximately 20 minutes

600-800 g piece of snoek
Coarse salt
Lemon wedges, baked sweet potato and a salad,
 to serve

Glaze
60 ml butter, melted
50 ml apricot jam
25 ml lemon juice
5 ml fish spice
1 small clove garlic, crushed
1 fresh chilli, seeded and chopped (optional)

1. Rub the snoek with salt and leave to stand for 30 minutes. Wash off the salt thoroughly and pat dry.
2. Mix the glaze ingredients together.
3. Place the snoek in an aluminium foil container or ovenproof dish and pour the glaze over it. Preheat the air fryer to 190 °C and then cook the snoek for 20 minutes, turning halfway through cooking. The flesh will be white and will flake apart easily with a fork when it is done.
4. Serve hot with lemon wedges, sweet potato and salad.

OSTRICH FRIKKADELS
with CHAKALAKA

Ostrich meat is a healthier local alternative to beef and tastes just as good! Serve these frikkadels with home-made or store-bought chakalaka as a flavoursome family meal.

Serves: 4
Preparation time: 30 minutes
Air-fryer temperature: 180 °C
Cooking time: approximately 20 minutes

2 slices of white bread, crusts removed
500 g ostrich mince
2 cloves garlic, crushed
½ onion, finely chopped
30 ml freshly chopped parsley
Pinch of ground cloves
5 ml ground coriander
1 ml ground turmeric
1 large egg
Salt and freshly ground black pepper, to taste
20 ml canola oil
410 g can mild or hot chakalaka, to serve
Pap or mashed potato and vegetables, to serve

1. Add a little water to the bread and allow to soak. Then squeeze dry. Put the bread into a bowl and add the mince, garlic, onion, parsley, spices and egg. Season well with salt and freshly ground black pepper. Mix well.
2. Shape into medium-sized balls using your hands. Flatten each one slightly.
3. Pour the oil onto a plate and then roll the meatballs in the oil to coat, or spray with oil if you have an oil spray bottle.
4. Preheat the air fryer to 180 °C. Place the frikkadels into the basket of the air fryer. Cook for 18-20 minutes, turning halfway through the cooking time.
5. Heat up the chakalaka and serve with the frikkadels. Accompany with *pap* or mashed potato and vegetables.

SAUCY ROOIBOS *and* GRANADILLA PUDDING

This sweet and sticky pudding is flavoured with rooibos and granadilla, and is a comforting after-dinner treat.

🍴 Serves: 6
🕐 Preparation time: 20 minutes
🌡️ Air-fryer temperature: 160 °C
⏱️ Cooking time: 35-40 minutes

4 rooibos tea bags
75 g (80 ml) soft butter
90 g (100 ml) castor sugar
1 large egg
Grated zest and juice of one lemon
75 g (140 ml) self-raising flour
110 g can granadilla pulp
10 ml cornflour
Icing sugar, to dust
Custard or cream, to serve

1. Put the rooibos tea bags into a jug and cover with 250 ml boiling water. Leave to steep.
2. Beat the butter, 70 g castor sugar and the egg together until light. Fold in the lemon zest, 15 ml lemon juice, the flour and granadilla pulp. Spoon into a greased aluminium foil container or ovenproof dish.
3. Mix the cornflour with the remaining lemon juice. Remove the rooibos bags from the jug and heat the tea in the microwave until just boiling. Add a little of the hot mixture to the lemon and cornflour mix and stir well, then add to the hot mixture and stir again. Pour over the batter in the dish.
4. Preheat the air fryer to 160 °C. Put the dish into the basket of the air fryer and cook for 35-40 minutes or until the pudding is firm and golden. Remove from the air fryer.
5. Allow to stand for 10 minutes, then dust with icing sugar and serve warm with custard or cream.

MILK
TART

Here's the air-fryer version of South Africa's favourite tea-time treat.

Serves: 6-8

Preparation time: 30 minutes,
   plus refrigeration time

Air-fryer temperature: 160 °C

Cooking time: approximately 60 minutes

1 roll ready-made shortcrust pastry

Filling
600 ml full-cream milk
2 cinnamon sticks
6 cardamom pods
90 g (100 ml) castor sugar
35 g (65 ml) cake flour
20 ml cornflour
Pinch of salt
40 g (45 ml) butter
3 large eggs
5 ml vanilla essence
Ground cinnamon or cinnamon sugar, to serve

1. Grease a 15-cm pie tin. Unroll the pastry onto a lightly floured surface and roll out lightly so it is a little thinner. Cut out a circle to line the pie tin, and large enough to allow a little excess pastry to hang over the sides slightly. Place the pastry into the pie dish and prick the base a few times with a fork. Refrigerate for 30 minutes.

2. Preheat the air fryer to 160 °C. Put the pie tin into the basket and cook for 15-20 minutes or until the pastry is firm and a light golden colour. Remove from the air fryer and cool. Use a sharp serrated knife to trim off the excess pastry to leave a neat edge.

3. **Filling:** Heat the milk with the cinnamon sticks and cardamom pods. In a bowl, stir the sugar, flour, cornflour and a pinch of salt together and set aside. Bring the milk to the boil, then reduce the heat and add the sugar and flour mixture, whisking well to prevent lumps. Cook, stirring, for 10 minutes until thickened. Remove the cinnamon sticks and cardamom pods. Add the butter.

4. Whisk in the eggs and vanilla.

5. Pour the filling into the prepeared crust and cook in the preheated air fryer at 160 °C for 25-30 minutes or until the filling is set, but still slightly wobbly. Set aside to cool.

6. Refrigerate until ready to serve. Serve sprinkled with cinnamon or cinnamon sugar.

MALVA
PUDDING

This much-loved South African pudding bakes very successfully in an air fryer.

 Serves: 6-8

Preparation time: 20 minutes

Air-fryer temperature: 160 °C

Cooking time: 25-30 minutes

85 g (155 ml) cake flour
5 ml bicarbonate of soda
1 large egg
110 g (125 ml) castor sugar
80 ml buttermilk
30 ml milk
7 ml vinegar
10 ml apricot jam
15 ml butter

Syrup
40 ml butter
60 ml sugar
60 ml cream
60 ml milk

1. Sift the flour and bicarbonate of soda together. Beat the egg and castor sugar together until light.
2. Heat the buttermilk, milk, vinegar, jam and butter together over a low heat. Once the ingredients have melted, remove from the heat and beat for a few seconds.
3. Fold the flour mixture, egg mixture and buttermilk mixture together. Spoon into a greased 15 x 20-cm aluminium foil tin.
4. Preheat the air fryer to 160 °C. Place the baking container into the air fryer basket and cook for 25-30 minutes or until firm and dark brown. Remove from the air fryer and set aside on a cooling rack.
5. **Syrup:** Heat the syrup ingredients together until melted. Pour over the baked pudding and allow to soak in. Serve warm with ice cream or custard.

BAKES *and* SWEET TREATS

Mosbolletjie
BREAD AND BUTTER PUDDING

 Serves: 4-6

 Preparation time: 15 minutes

Air-fryer temperature: 160 °C

Cooking time: 15-20 minutes

50 ml soft butter
30 ml apricot jam
½ mosbolletjie bread loaf, sliced
30 ml chopped dried apricots
Handful of fresh raspberries
110 ml milk
110 ml cream
2 large eggs

An easy pudding to make with lovely aniseed and fruity berry flavours.

1. Mix the butter and apricot jam together and spread onto the slices of bread.
2. Grease an aluminium container or ovenproof dish and then layer the slices of bread in the container. Scatter the chopped apricots and raspberries in between the layers.
3. Whisk the milk, cream and eggs together and pour over the bread. Leave to soak in for 5 minutes.
4. Preheat the air fryer to 160 °C. Put the container into the basket of the air fryer and cook for 15-20 minutes until set and golden. Serve hot with whipped cream or custard.

CHOCOLATE CARAMEL
PEPPERMINT CRISP CAKE

Everyone will love this rich, dark chocolate cake topped with caramel and Peppermint Crisp. You can make half the quantity if you need a smaller, single-layer cake.

🍴 Makes: 2 x 15-cm round cakes

🕐 Preparation time: 30 minutes

🌡️ Air-fryer temperature: 160 °C

⏱️ Cooking time: approximately 35 minutes per layer

80 g (240 ml) cocoa powder
2 ml bicarbonate of soda
4 large eggs
370 g (420 ml) brown sugar
180 ml sunflower oil
200 g (370 ml) self-raising flour
360 g can caramel treat
1 Peppermint Crisp chocolate bar, crushed

1. Put the cocoa powder into a bowl and add 200 ml boiling water. Stir until smooth. Add the bicarbonate of soda and stir well. Set aside to cool.
2. Beat the eggs, sugar and oil together and then stir in the flour and the cocoa mixture.
3. Grease and line two 15-cm round cake tins. Divide the batter equally between the tins. (You can also use two 15 x 20-cm rectangular aluminium containers if you would like a tray bake.)
4. Preheat the air fryer to 160 °C. Place one tin into the basket of the air fryer and cook for 30-35 minutes. To test, a skewer inserted should come out clean.
5. Remove from the air fryer and cool on a baking rack. Cook the remaining batter and then cool.
6. Once the cakes are cool, trim the tops so they are flatter. Sandwich together with caramel. Top with the remaining caramel and sprinkle with crushed Peppermint Crisp. Store in an airtight container.

KOESISTER
CUPCAKES

These lightly spiced coconut-topped cupcakes borrow their flavours from the Cape Malay favourite, koesisters.

🍴 Makes: 12 cupcakes

🕐 Preparation time: 30 minutes

🌡️ Air-fryer temperature: 180 °C

⏱️ Cooking time: approximately 40 minutes

115 g (125 ml) soft butter
170 g (195 ml) castor sugar
2 large eggs
270 g (500 ml) self-raising flour
4 ml each ground cardamom, cinnamon,
  aniseed and ginger
200 ml milk
40 g (125 ml) desiccated coconut, for sprinkling

Icing
100 g (110 ml) soft butter
250 g (480 ml) icing sugar, sifted
1 ml each ground cinnamon and ground cardamom
5 ml vanilla essence
20 ml milk

1. Line silicone cupcake holders with cupcake papers. Beat the butter and sugar together until light. Add the eggs, one at a time, beating well after each addition.

2. Sift the flour and spices together. Fold the flour into the butter mixture, alternating with the milk. Spoon into the prepared cases so that they are three-quarters full.

3. Preheat the air fryer to 180 °C. Put a layer of cupcakes into the air fryer. Cover the cupcakes with a piece of aluminium foil, tucking the sides of the foil over them so that it doesn't blow upwards when the air fryer is on. Cook for 10 minutes at 180 °C. Remove the foil and continue to cook for further 5-10 minutes or until a skewer inserted comes out clean. Remove from the air fryer and place onto a cooling rack. Bake the remaining cupcakes.

4. **Icing:** Beat the butter until light. Add the icing sugar, spices and vanilla and beat well. Add enough milk to form a spreadable consistency. Spread or pipe onto the cooled cupcakes and sprinkle with coconut. Store in an airtight container.

CHOC-NUT
BROWNIES

These chocolate brownies are easy to bake in an air fryer and make a decadent after-dinner treat or a special home-made gift.

Makes: 30 brownies
Preparation time: 30 minutes
Air-fryer temperature: 160 °C
Cooking time: 25-30 minutes

125 g (135 ml) butter
45 g (140 ml) cocoa powder
2 large eggs
200 g (230 ml) castor sugar
5 ml vanilla extract
150 g (275 ml) self-raising flour
60 g (70 ml) dark chocolate, chopped
60 g (130 ml) pecan nuts or hazelnuts, chopped

1. Melt the butter. Remove from the heat and stir in the cocoa.
2. Beat the eggs until light, add the sugar and vanilla and beat well. Stir in the cocoa mixture.
3. Sift the flour and fold in, along with three-quarters of the chocolate and nuts.
4. Pour into a greased 15 x 20-cm aluminium container. Sprinkle the remaining chocolate and nuts on top of the batter.
5. Preheat the air fryer to 160 °C. Once it is hot, place the baking container into the basket of the air fryer. Bake for 25-30 minutes. The mixture should be just set, but still a little soft in the middle. Don't be tempted to overcook it. It will firm up after it cools and should remain slightly soft and gooey in the middle.
6. Remove from the oven and cool on a baking tray. Once it is cold, use a sharp knife to cut into squares. Store in an airtight container.

CRUNCHIES

Always a favourite, whether you're young or old, these oat crunchies are ready in no time when baked in an air fryer.

Makes: 20 crunchies

Preparation time: 20 minutes

Air-fryer temperature: 160 °C

Cooking time: approximately 35 minutes

75 g (140 ml) cake flour
75 g (180 ml) rolled oats
75 g (240 ml) desiccated coconut
85 g (100 ml) sugar
5 ml ground cinnamon
Pinch of salt
45 g (60 ml) golden syrup
65 g (70 ml) butter
1 ml bicarbonate of soda
30 ml milk

1. Grease a 15 x 20-cm rectangular aluminium foil container. Combine the flour, oats, coconut, sugar, cinnamon and a large pinch of salt in a mixing bowl.
2. Melt the syrup and butter together. Combine the bicarbonate of soda with the milk and then stir into the butter mixture. Pour into the dry ingredients and stir well.
3. Preheat the air fryer to 160 °C. Press the mixture into the greased container. Bake for 30-35 minutes until dark golden brown. Remove from the air fryer and allow to cool for 20 minutes before slicing into pieces.
4. Cool completely and then store in an airtight container.

BRAN
MUFFINS

You can make the batter for this muffin recipe in advance and keep it in an airtight container in the fridge for up to 30 days. Bake a batch of muffins in the morning for breakfast or to pop into the kids' lunchboxes. You can always have fresh muffins on hand!

Makes: 24 muffins
Preparation time: 15 minutes
Air-fryer temperature: 180 °C
Baking time: 15-20 minutes per batch

2 large eggs
125 ml canola oil
250 g (290 ml) brown sugar
350 g (645 ml) cake flour
70 g (375 ml) digestive bran
5 ml salt
5 ml vanilla essence
10 ml bicarbonate of soda
190 g (250 ml) raisins or other dried fruit
140 ml (150 g) seedless dates, chopped

Topping
65 g (160 ml) oats
35 g (40 ml) brown sugar
35 g (60 ml) cake flour
45 g (50 ml) butter

1. Whisk the eggs, oil and sugar together. Add the remaining ingredients.
2. Rub the topping ingredients together to form a crumble.
3. Line silicone muffin holders with baking papers or use muffin cups. Fill to three-quarters full with the bran mixture. Spoon a little of the crumble mixture onto each one.
4. Preheat the air fryer to 180 °C. Put a layer of muffins into the basket of the air fryer and cover loosely with aluminium foil. Tuck the sides of the foil over so it won't fly upwards when the air fryer is on. Close the air fryer and cook for 15-20 minutes or until a skewer inserted comes out clean. Cool and store in an airtight container.

HERTZOGGIE
SLICES

Bake this popular South African cookie in your air fryer and enjoy for afternoon tea.

Makes: 16 slices

Preparation time: 30 minutes

Air-fryer temperature: 160 °C

Cooking time: approximately 25 minutes

100 g (180 ml) cake flour
3 ml baking powder
Pinch of salt
60 g (65 ml) butter
30 ml castor sugar
2 large eggs, separated
60 ml smooth apricot jam
80 g (90 ml) castor sugar
80 g (255 ml) desiccated coconut

1. Sift the flour and baking powder together with a pinch of salt. Rub in the butter and add the castor sugar. Whisk the egg yolks and stir into the mixture to make a dough.
2. Press evenly over the base of a greased 15 x 20-cm aluminium foil container. Prick all over the base with a fork.
3. Spread the apricot jam over the pastry. Preheat the air fryer to 160 °C. Place the aluminium tin into the basket of the air fryer and cook for 8 minutes.
4. Meanwhile, prepare the topping. Beat the egg whites together until stiff. Stir in the sugar and coconut.
5. Remove the tin from the air fryer and spoon the topping over the jam. Return to the air fryer and bake for 12-15 minutes at 160 °C until the topping is crisp and light golden. Remove from the air fryer and cool completely.
6. Use a sharp knife to cut into slices. Store in an airtight container.

CHEESE *and*
SPRING ONION BREAD

A yummy starter snack to serve at a braai, or serve with a bowl of vegetable soup. If you're short on time, buy ready-made bread dough instead of making your own.

🍴 Serves: 6-8

🕐 Preparation time: 20 minutes, plus rising time

🌡️ Air-fryer temperature: 160 °C

⏱️ Baking time: approximately 30 minutes

Dough
340 g (625 ml) white bread flour
5 ml salt
5 g instant dry yeast
120 ml warm water

Filling
40 g (45 ml) soft butter
30 ml finely chopped fresh parsley
1 clove garlic, crushed
4 spring onions, sliced
Salt, to taste
20 g (35 ml) grated Parmesan
25 g (55 ml) grated white Cheddar cheese

1. **Dough:** Sift the flour, salt and yeast into a large bowl. Add the water and stir to combine. Knead for 10 minutes. Once the dough is smooth and elastic, roll it into a ball and place into a large bowl. Cover with a damp tea towel. Set aside to rise for about 2 hours or until doubled in size.

2. **Filling:** Stir the butter, parsley, garlic and spring onions together. Season with salt.

3. Knead down the dough. Roll it out onto a lightly floured surface so that it forms a rectangle.

4. Spread the filling over the dough and then sprinkle with the cheeses. Roll up the dough so it forms a long roll. Use a sharp knife to cut into 6-8 even-sized rounds.

5. Place the rounds into a greased 15 x 20-cm aluminium baking container.

6. Preheat the air fryer to 160 °C. Place the container into the air fryer basket and cook for 25-30 minutes. Serve warm.

WAFFLES *with* AMARULA
CARAMEL APPLES

A scrumptious dessert to end off your meal in style.

🍴 Serves: 4
🕐 Preparation time: 20 minutes
🌡 Air-fryer temperature: 160 °C
⏱ Cooking time: approximately 30 minutes

3 Pink Lady or Granny Smith apples,
    cored and cut into wedges
5 ml lemon juice
5 ml ground cinnamon
25 ml cake flour
100 g (110 ml) white sugar
40 g (45 ml) brown sugar
60 ml Amarula liqueur
30 ml cold butter, cut into small pieces
4 ready-made waffles, to serve
Ice cream, to serve
45 ml flaked almonds, toasted, to serve
Fresh strawberries, to serve

1. Put the apple wedges into a bowl and add the lemon juice, cinnamon, flour, sugars and Amarula and stir well. Place in an aluminium foil or ovenproof dish. Add the butter.
2. Preheat the air fryer to 160 °C. Put the dish into the air fryer basket and cook for 20-25 minutes until the apples are tender. Stir halfway through the cooking time. Remove from the air fryer.
3. Increase the air fryer temperature to 180 °C. Put the waffles into the air fryer basket and cook for 6 minutes. Turn halfway through. You may need to do two batches if they don't all fit in the air fryer together.
4. Serve the waffles hot, topped with a scoop of ice cream and the Amarula apples. Sprinkle with almonds and garnish with strawberries.

INDEX

*Page numbers in **bold italic** refer to photos*

ACKNOWLEDGEMENTS

· ·

A special thank you to Dad, Mom, Vati, Mutti, Dani, Michael, Ben and my friends who are always there to support me and are always enthusiastic about the food I cook. Thanks for being the willing taste-testers and for putting up with a slightly chaotic house full of food, props and air fryers during the production of this book.

A huge thanks to the food team for your hard work and for making shoot days so much fun. Thanks, Donna, for the gorgeous photos, and Hannes for all the support, creative input, inspiration and fabulous food styling.

And last but not least, thanks very much to Human & Rousseau and the whole team who worked on this book, especially Lindy – it has been a real pleasure working with you.